# IT'S TIME 2 HEAL

## Healing the Hole in Your Soul

*A life-changing* ~~guide~~ *al from* ~~the~~

Merry P. Ware, LPC, NCC

ISBN 978-1-950861-60-6

PRINTED IN THE UNTIED STATES OF AMERICA

His Glory Creations Publishing, LLC
Wendell, North Carolina

# ACKNOWLEDGEMENTS

To God be the Glory. I give Him all the honor, glory, and praise!

To my husband, Robert, my best friend, thank you for all of your love and support. You have always shown me that you are truly my #1 fan and you have ALWAYS had my back.

To my lovely daughters, Robyn and Merissa, thank you for all the words of encouragement. I pray that I will always make both of you proud.

To my mother, Helen, thank you for instilling in me the importance of prayer and always keeping God first in my life. You are a true example of what it means to be a woman of God.

# Table of Contents

# Introduction

Welcome to the beginning of a life-changing journey. Congratulations for choosing this moment as 'YOUR' Time 2 Heal. As you work through this book you will learn more about abuse, the impact it has on your life, and how to move forward toward healing through self-acceptance and self-love. This book was designed to increase awareness and knowledge, which are the first steps toward change and growth, so that you no longer live in the pain of the abuse. You will discover your worth, your value, and the freedom that you deserve. The exercises and reflections were created to help you explore and enhance your own needs and desires for happiness.

At times, this may not be an easy journey, but it is one that is long overdue. If it feels challenging while you are making your way through this book, just remember the discomfort is only temporary and is not designed to hinder your journey. I encourage you to be patient and kind with yourself as you embark on this journey toward healing. You have made the best decision to take control of your life, your happiness, and your peace. Let's get started on the road to healing.

# CHAPTER 1

# Understanding Abuse

Sometimes terrible things happen to us and we question whether it really happened or if it was really abuse. If you were hurt by someone who you loved or someone you *thought* loved you, you may be wondering if it was abuse. Sometimes it may be difficult to gauge if those things or occurrences were considered abuse, especially if they happened in your childhood.

You may be wondering about certain situations, or even asking yourself questions such as, "Could those hurtful things my parents did or said to me be considered abuse?", "Could that unwanted touch from my cousin or uncle be considered abuse?", "Could the terrible thing that happened to me, which I never told anyone about, be considered abuse?" The answer is probably YES.

Abuse comes in many forms, such as childhood abuse, sexual abuse, and domestic violence, however, there are other types of abuse. Oftentimes, we have a misconception of the term 'abuse,' so let's start by defining the word abuse.

Abuse is any behavior intended to control, threaten, intimidate, or hurt someone. It can be emotional, psychological, sexual, physical, financial, and even spiritual. Any unwanted or uncomfortable experience is considered abuse. Any misuse of power to control you is considered abuse. Now that you are clear on the definition, you can become clear about answers to the questions above. The answer is YES to those things that you were wondering about. Yes, they are considered abuse.

## Types of Abuse

*Emotional Abuse* – This type of abuse is the hardest to identify, mainly because it can be subtle and there is no physical evidence. Since abuse is most commonly associated with being physically harmed, you may feel that you are not being abused because you were never hit, pushed, or grabbed. Many people feel that way, which is why emotional abuse is under-reported, or never reported, by the victim.

It is important that you understand that abuse is about control, therefore, emotional abuse can be used to control you in a similar way as physical abuse. With emotional abuse, the perpetrator uses his/her words instead of his/her hands. The abuser uses words as a weapon to make you feel less than by demeaning you, isolating you, or belittling you, all in an effort to control YOU.

## Signs of Emotional Abuse

Check any of these signs that you have experienced

- ☐ Calls you insulting names (i.e., stupid, disgusting, worthless)
- ☐ Acts very jealous, including constantly accusing you of cheating
- ☐ Threatens to hurt your children, your family, or your pets
- ☐ Threatens to harm himself/herself when they get upset with you

*Financial Abuse* – Financial abuse is when a partner/spouse controls money in a relationship in a way that withholds funds from the victim. It is all about controlling your resources (cash, credit cards, bank accounts). If the person controls your resources, that person can control you.

## Signs of Financial Abuse

Check any of these signs that you have experienced

- ☐ The abuser takes your paychecks or restricts you to an allowance; they only give you a certain amount of money to spend, regardless of your request for more
- ☐ The abuser hides financial information from you, such as bank accounts and assets. This is also known as financial infidelity because it is kept a secret to the victim
- ☐ The abuser tells you that you are unintelligent or incapable of managing your own money, which is the abuser's way of justifying their control of the finances in the relationship
- ☐ Constantly questioning your purchases, demanding to see receipts, and asking you things such as, "When did you buy that?", or "How much did that cost?"

*Spiritual Abuse* – This type of abuse can be very difficult to talk about for many people. It is probably the most misunderstood than any other type of abuse. With spiritual abuse the person uses religion as their weapon. The perpetrator can be a religious leader, parent, or a spouse. Spiritual abuse can occur when a person/group uses spiritual authority, leadership, biblical scriptures, or spiritual based threats, to exercise power and control over you.

## Signs of Spiritual Abuse

Check any of these signs that you have experienced

- ☐ Scriptures were used to manipulate, condemn, or humiliate you
- ☐ Pressured to give money that you didn't have to give
- ☐ Religious beliefs were used to control your clothing, behavior, or decision making
- ☐ You were made to believe or feel that you were not worthy of God's love and grace
- ☐ Religion was used to justify abuse

*Psychological Abuse* – The abuser likes to play mind games with his/her victim. So, he/she uses a manipulation technique, commonly known as 'gas lighting', to undermine your perception of reality. It is used by the abuser to deflect the blame for the abusive behavior in order to point the finger at you. Gas lighting is when the abuser psychologically manipulates you into questioning your own sanity. In other words, the abuser makes you feel like you are losing your mind. The perpetrator uses these types of abuse to take away your independence and confidence. This helps the abuser to maintain power and control in the relationship.

## Signs of Psychological Abuse

Check any of these signs that you have experienced

- ☐ You constantly second-guess yourself
- ☐ You feel inadequate, like you are never "good enough"
- ☐ You're always apologizing to your partner
- ☐ You feel as though you cannot do anything right

*Childhood Abuse* – This type of abuse occurs in many forms and can vary from mild to severe.

## Types of Childhood Abuse

Check any of these types of childhood abuse that you have experienced

- ☐ Child sexual abuse – This includes fondling, oral contact, and touching of private parts in anyway. (Boys can be victims of sexual abuse, however, girls are 3 times more likely to experience sexual abuse and to be abused by a family member or family friend.)

- ☐ Child physical abuse – Girls and boys are equally likely to be physically abused. Parents and even siblings can be abusive.

- ☐ Emotional and verbal abuse – This kind of abuse is often disguised as humor in a family, such as calling someone 'out of their name', comparing one sibling to another, or making mean comments. It also includes intentionally embarrassing a child in the presence of his/her friends or even strangers.

- ☐ Neglect – This is the failure to properly provide food, clothing, or a safe environment for a child. It also includes not taking a child to the doctor when needed.

# Stages of Abuse

Just as there are several types of abuse there are also various stages of abuse. We will start with the stages first and then take a look at recommendations for help and support for each stage.

## Stage 1: Uncertainty

This is when you are unsure that the pain you suffered is a form of abuse. Uncertainty can also occur when you know that something bad or terrible happened to you in your past, but you are unable to recall the details.

## Stage 2: Victim

If you are currently in an abusive relationship or have recently experienced an abusive situation, you would be in the victim stage.

## Stage 3: 3Ds (Denial, Diminish, and Detachment)

*Denial* is when you are being abused and you do not believe that you are, or you are not willing to accept that you are being abused. You may make statements such as, "Nothing happened. I don't know what you're talking about."

*Diminish* is a way of minimizing the abuse; it is when you are being abused, yet you make excuses for the abuser. You may make statements such as, "He *only* pushes me and *maybe once*, he slapped me", "He didn't mean to give me a black eye."

*Detachment* is when you become emotionally numb to the abuse. You may feel disconnected and may begin isolating yourself from others.

## Stage 4: Survivor

This is when you believe or say things like, "I'm making it, I'm okay." You have put the abuse in the back of your mind and moved on (*well that's what you tell yourself*), but you have never emotionally healed, therefore you still struggle with the feelings associated with the abuse: shame, guilt, low self-esteem, loneliness, anger, resentment, trust issues, and difficulty maintaining healthy relationships.

## Stage 5: Victory – (Healing phase)

The Healing Phase is when you can tell your story without reliving the pain of the past. It's when you come to the point where you realize that your past does not *define* you, rather it *prepares* you for your purpose.

Victory is a state of mind; it is when you have joy and peace. You are able to have healthy and meaningful relationships. Victory is being able to celebrate your true and authentic self. The victory stage is where you gain a sense of empowerment by no longer seeing yourself as a victim. It is when you can see beyond *just surviving* and begin seeing yourself living life to the fullest.

## Recommendations

A recommendation for **ANY** stage, if you feel you are in any danger, call 911 or your local police department.

Recommendations for the uncertainty stage – Review the chapter 'Understanding Abuse' again to seek clarification. Talk to someone you trust to get their opinion. If you are alone right now, and have no one to talk to, you can trust that still, quiet voice inside you that is telling you that you were abused and that you are on the right track to begin healing.

Recommendations for the victim stage – If you are in immediate danger, call 911. Tell someone you trust. Create a safety plan to ensure that you are in a safe position to remove yourself from the abusive environment or situation. This may include going to a shelter, a safe house, or staying with family or a close friend. Remember you MUST have a plan!

<u>Recommendations for the 3Ds stage</u> – It is important to acknowledge and recognize that the abuse did occur. You must understand that it was not your fault. Abuse is never the victim's fault. You may want to seek individual counseling, group therapy, or spiritual guidance.

<u>Recommendations for the survivor</u> – Recognize relationship patterns, work on loving yourself, and increasing self-esteem. You may want to join a support group, attend seminars on empowerment and self-worth, get a life coach, or seek spiritual guidance or counseling.

<u>Recommendations for the victory stage</u> – Congratulations for making it to this stage. It is time to encourage others, give back, volunteer, and share your gifts. It is time for you to begin walking in your passion and purpose for your life.

# Exercise:

Take a look at the scenario below and see if you can identify Janet's stage of abuse. Janet has been in an abusive relationship with her boyfriend for over a year. The abuse started out as emotional abuse and has progressed to physical abuse.

Janet was at a restaurant with her best friend Michelle. Michelle noticed a bruise on Janet's arm. Michelle asked, "Janet, is everything ok with you?" Janet slowly began talking about her relationship. She stated "Well, we argue sometimes, like all couples do, but he only pushed me one time and it really wasn't that hard."

*What stage is Janet in?* _____

Answer: **3Ds stage**

Reason: Janet is in the 3Ds stage of **Diminish** because she is minimizing the abuse. Notice her words: *but he only pushed me one time and it really wasn't that hard.*

If you feel that you are in a safe space and are ready to examine where you are in the stages of abuse, see the steps below to begin now. If, for any reason, you are not ready or feel uncomfortable, you should revisit this exercise at a later time.

If you are ready, you may begin. Take a moment to identify which stage best describes you and then consider some of the recommendations for that stage.

*What stage of abuse do you consider yourself to be in at this moment? What events helped you to make that determination?*

_____

_____

_____

_____

*What steps can you try from the list of recommendations?*

_____

_____

_____

_____

CHAPTER 2

# The Impact of Abuse and Trauma

Some people are greatly impacted by their past abuse, while others may not have any symptoms at all. It is also possible to fall somewhere in between. Some factors that may play a part in this is whether you knew, trusted, or were emotionally attached to the person.

When it comes to sexual abuse, severity is a major factor and is determined by the magnitude of the victim's experiences. Physical abuse is characterized by degree, meaning the more severe the abuse, the worse the injuries. Neglect is characterized by the degree of deficiency. In general, abuse that occurs more frequently and lasts longer will be more damaging than abuse that was infrequent and occurred in a shorter amount of time.

Severe childhood abuse can have a long-term impact on how you function emotionally and interact with others. It can cause you to have trust issues or see the world as unsafe. The feelings of betrayal that you experienced in childhood may manifest into your adulthood, causing significant impact on your relationships.

Abuse and trauma are related because the impact of abuse can lead to trauma, however, everyone who has experienced abuse may not be traumatized. Trauma is unique to each individual. Trauma is subjective. The victim is the one who gets to determine if the abuse was traumatic. Trauma is defined as the exposure to, or witnessing of, a difficult or unpleasant experience that has a lasting negative impact on your thoughts, feelings, or behavior. Trauma can be described as your inability to cope emotionally or psychologically because of the abuse you have experienced.

Trauma can impact all areas of your life: emotionally, physically, or even socially. Some common reactions to trauma are headaches, a rapid heartbeat, irritability, fear, sadness, and difficulty concentrating. In most cases, trauma symptoms will gradually fade as you process the unsettling events. You will be able to go on with your life without experiencing any lasting negative effects. There are some survivors that experience normal traumatic stress reactions, however it does not impact their mental health, due to their resiliency skills and their strong support system.

For other survivors, their trauma reactions may not ease up, instead they become worse. They begin to notice that they are not able to move on from the event and continually experience traumatic stress reactions. These reactions could potentially develop into Post-Traumatic Stress Disorder (PTSD).

PTSD is a mental health condition defined as a severe and long-term condition associated with high levels of ongoing distress that causes significant impairment in a person's daily life. It is important to understand that you can experience normal trauma reactions and NOT develop PTSD. Seeking help and support can also prevent your trauma reactions from getting worse and developing into PTSD.

With PTSD a person can experience symptoms immediately or it could take weeks, months, or even years to develop. PTSD symptoms are described in clusters such as:

- *Re-experiencing* - nightmares and flashbacks
- *Avoidance* - avoiding activities and places that remind you of the trauma or avoiding thoughts and feelings relating to the trauma

- *Arousal/Reactivity* - being super alert, feeling on edge, or being easily startled
- *Mood/cognition symptoms* - difficulty feeling positive emotions or negative or distorted thoughts about yourself or the world

Naturally coping can help the symptoms to lessen gradually as opposed to coping in unhealthy ways. Examples of unhealthy coping is withdrawing and isolating from loved ones and using drugs or alcohol. If your traumatic experience is just too painful and powerful for you to manage alone, you may need professional help.

Unfortunately, there are still negative stigmas associated with getting professional help. Please do not allow any stigmas to stop you from getting the help that you need. I want you to know that it is OK to get help from a professional. Getting help can start with a conversation. Simply talking to a professional can be beneficial. Trained mental health professionals, who can help you deal with PTSD, are counselors, therapists, psychologists, or psychiatrists. Addressing your mental health is just as important as addressing your physical health.

CHAPTER 3

# Creating Safety

Everyone deserves and needs to feel safe. For anyone involved in an abusive relationship, safety is always the number one priority. If you currently fear for your safety, please seek immediate help. For those of you who have experienced an abusive relationship or traumatic event in the past, the need to feel safe is still the number one priority. Even though there may not be a current threat of danger, your past situation may have robbed you of your sense of safety.

Safety can be defined in many ways because it is individualized and personalized. It could mean having someone in your life to protect you. For others, feeling safe means having a good escape plan. Yet for others, safety could mean relying on you to protect yourself.

There arc three components of feeling safe:

1. Being safe with yourself.
2. Being safe with others.
3. Being safe out in the world.

## Being safe with yourself.

Creating safety for yourself is an individual process and therefore you need to identify what makes you feel safe.

## Exercise:

Which of the following positive and supportive things do you already have in your life?

☐ A compassionate person
☐ An item that brings you comfort
☐ An uplifting song that makes you feel good
☐ A place that makes you happy

*When you think of safety what type of feelings occur? What kinds of images do you think of? What makes you feel protected?*

_____

_____

_____

Grounding, also known as centering, is another way to help you feel safe. It involves a set of strategies to help you deal with emotional pain when it feels overwhelming. Grounding anchors you to the present moment which helps you to focus outward rather than inward to yourself. Grounding can be thought of as a healthy distraction or your personal safe place.

There are three types of grounding: mental, physical, and soothing. Mental is when you focus on your mind. Physical is when you focus on your senses. Soothing is when you speak to yourself in a kind way.

*Examples of Mental grounding*

- *Describe your environment in detail*
- *Describe items, textures, colors, and shapes*
- *Count to 10 slowly or backwards (10, 9, 8,...etc.)*

*Examples of Physical grounding*

- *Carry a grounding object with you that you can touch whenever you feel emotionally triggered (small stone, symbolic object, piece of cloth, etc.)*
- *Stretch - extend your arms and legs as far as you can*
- *Clench and release your fists*

*Examples of Soothing Grounding*

- *Say kind statements, as if you were talking to a friend; for example, "You are a good person going through a rough moment, you can get through this"*
- *Listen to soothing music*
- *Remember the words to an inspiring song, poem, or quotation, which makes you feel better*

When it comes to grounding or centering, all three types are helpful, however try to notice which ones work better for you. Remember to start using your grounding/centering techniques before your emotions get out of control.

## Being safe with other people.

It is important to be safe during your interactions with others. As a survivor of abuse, you may no longer have the relationships that once existed. You may feel misunderstood or unsafe with people you once felt safe being around. As a result, you may find yourself in need of friends and healthy relationships. It would be beneficial to join a support group with others dealing with similar situations. In this type of setting, you will meet supportive people to talk to and connect with. Perhaps later, the acquaintanceship may turn into friendship.

You can also talk to someone in the helping profession who can provide the safe space that you need. Remember, you need to feel safe in at least one relationship while you heal and find ways to connect and build healthy relationships with others.

## Being safe out in the world.

It is important to be safe as you move around in the physical world. After experiencing a traumatic event, your feelings of safety may be replaced with fear and anxiety. Setting boundaries is a fantastic way to create safety. Boundaries are limits that you set regarding what you will and will not accept from others.

As a survivor, your boundaries were violated, whether the abuser was someone you knew or a stranger. Any type of abuse is a boundary invasion. One of the most common struggles survivors of abuse face is learning how to set healthy boundaries. When you set and enforce boundaries, you are choosing to take action and create safety for yourself.

We discover our physical comfort zones through our physical boundaries. Having healthy physical boundaries allows you to determine how close others get to you, when you want to be touched, and who you will allow to touch you. It means YOU *give* that right to others.

## Exercise:

*How much space do you need? What is a comfortable distance between you and others?*

_____

(*i.e., Arm's length*)

*How do you react to unwanted contact?*

_____

(*i.e., Get angry, feel anxious, walk-away*)

*How does your body language say stay away or come close?*

_____

(*i.e., Folding your arms, turning you head, making eye contact, smiling etc.*)

It is important to know your physical comfort zones and boundaries. Unfortunately for survivors, this may be a struggle because a traumatic experience can leave a person wavering between boundary extremes. For example, isolation vs. instant attachment, submission vs. dominance, or giving too much vs. giving too little. These are common boundary extremes. You need to learn how to set healthy boundaries and avoid extremes.

Give yourself permission to create healthy boundaries. Not only do you deserve them but recognize how much better your life will be with them.

DEFINE your boundaries: Think about:

*What upsets you or offends you?*

_____

_____

*Which person does this to you?*

_____

Most times it is the same person who crosses your boundaries.

Most people only think of safety in terms of physical safety; however, victims of abuse and trauma also need emotional safety. Survivors of abuse and trauma may struggle with saying no to the demands of others. They worry that they will be hurt or that they may disappoint others. They may also worry about abandonment or being disliked by others, which often means they lack healthy emotional boundaries.

Healthy emotional boundaries can be viewed as an internal shield or armor of protection. Emotional boundaries distinguish where your feelings end and where someone else's feelings begin. You must learn to take responsibility for your feelings and needs and allow others to do the same.

Many survivors of abuse tend to be people-pleasers. As a people-pleaser, you have the tendency to want to say yes to making others happy, regardless of how it makes you feel. This is definitely not okay. This opens the door for people to take advantage of you. You must identify when your boundaries are being crossed. To do that, you must recognize and stay tuned-in to your feelings. Take notice of any feelings of discomfort, anxiety, guilt, fear, or resentment. If you notice any of these discomforting signs, understand that what you are experiencing stems from feeling taken advantage of or not feeling appreciated.

Setting healthy emotional boundaries means that you no longer change who you are in order to be liked or accepted by someone. It means that you let go of the need to be needed, as well as your dependence on people for their approval. It also means that you commit to letting go of fixing, saving, or rescuing others.

## Exercise:

Start setting your emotional boundaries:

*I now let go of the need to fix*_____

_____

*I will no longer take responsibility for the outcome of*_____

_____

*I will no longer try to change myself for*_____

_____

Without setting healthy boundaries, people may disrespect or mistreat you. As you begin setting boundaries, you may notice some people will try to test you and your boundaries. Especially if these people were responsible for controlling, abusing, or manipulating you. Plan on it and expect it. You must stay firm with your boundaries and your actions should match up with the boundaries you are setting. You cannot successfully create clear boundaries if you send mixed messages, meaning you are apologizing to others for setting boundaries. You do not have to apologize, instead you need to be firm, clear, and respectful.

# CHAPTER 4

# Releasing

This could possibly be one of the hardest chapters in this book. Why, you ask. Because releasing involves forgiving and most people find it difficult to forgive others. One reason most people resist forgiveness is because they do not fully understand what it truly is and how it works. Some people assume that if you forgive someone, it means that you are letting that person off the hook. While others believe that forgiveness means you have to be friendly with the offender or abuser. No, that is not the case.

Forgiveness **is for you,** NOT the other person. Forgiveness **does not** mean that you excuse the offense or the offender. Forgiveness does not mean forgetting or denying that something bad or hurtful happened to you. I hope that after reading this you now have a better understanding of forgiveness. I hope that now, you are able to see that forgiveness is not something that you do for other people, forgiveness is something that you do for yourself.

Another important part of releasing is forgiving yourself. Unfortunately, many times we beat ourselves up for things that were not our fault or things that were out of our control. It's important that you realize that you are never the reason, the cause, or the blame for any of the abusive things that happened to you. For people who find it hard to understand this, it's easier for them to forgive others than it is for them to *forgive themselves*. If this is you, then please stop blaming yourself. You should not blame yourself for what you did not know. You did the best that you could *at that time*. Please give yourself permission to *forgive yourself*.

Forgiveness also opens the door to releasing. Releasing is another pivotal step in your healing process. By releasing the heaviness, the negativity, or emotional baggage, you are able to remove the weight that you have been carrying around that is weighing you down. Releasing is taking action to make space in your heart for what you really want in your life such as peace, love, and happiness.

There are many things that may be holding you back, which you might not be aware of, such as shame, guilt, hurt, resentment, or disappointment. You could be angry with yourself. For example, if you were in an abusive relationship, you may be angry at yourself for staying too long. You may be holding on to frustration because you felt that you should have known better or be angry at yourself because you didn't see it coming.

When you don't release negative energy, you are just keeping it bottled up inside. This can cause you to become bitter or explode emotionally. One of the best ways to release negative emotions is to write down your feelings. Writing about your feelings helps you to acknowledge them, process them and then release them. This can be done through poetry or even writing a letter to the person that hurt you and **NOT** sending it. Instead of sending it, you can shred it or burn it as a form of symbolic releasing.

Without releasing the heaviness or negativity that you are holding onto there will be no room in your heart for the positive things that you need to help you heal. It is important that you do not allow your heart to remain filled with things that are holding you back and keeping you stuck. The releasing comes by no longer holding on to it or allowing it to have a hold on you.

*What are some of the things that you need to release in your life that have a hold on you and are keeping you from moving forward?*

_____

_____

_____

# CHAPTER 5

# Reclaiming

The reclaiming of self is a necessary part of healing. Many people who have experienced abuse tend to struggle with knowing themselves. They may have low self-esteem and lack self-worth and value. When you do not believe in yourself, it is hard to see how you could be worthy of love or worthy of happiness, especially if you have been in a relationship where there was emotional or physical abuse. It can be hard to believe in yourself when the person who was supposed to love, cherish, and protect you, instead, spent their time breaking you down and destroying you.

Reclaiming yourself involves rediscovering yourself. It is vital that you take time to find out who you are, what you enjoy, your favorite foods, and even the kind of music that you like. Take some time to date yourself.

Take yourself out to a nice restaurant. Learn to enjoy yourself and celebrate yourself. Spend some quality time alone – what I call 'ME' time. Examples of 'me' time would be taking a long warm bubble bath, curling up in your favorite chair with a delightful book, or drinking a nice cup of tea.

Reclaiming yourself also involves learning to accept yourself and your uniqueness. Stop comparing yourself to others. There is always going to be someone who is smarter than you, in better shape than you, or perhaps, has a nicer body than you, SO WHAT? That's OK. Stop going around saying things such as "I wish I had her looks" or "I wish I had her anointing." Instead focus on your strengths and what makes you unique.

We are all created uniquely different. We all have different gifts and talents. We all have different thumb prints, mine are different from yours. There are no two fingerprints alike, just like there are no two snowflakes that are alike. You are your own unique person, and you have characteristics and strengths that no one else has. You need to truly understand that and believe it in your heart. *Well, how do I do that?* You have to get it into your spirit. Affirmations can be used as a way to remind yourself just how special and beautiful you are and that you are worthy of love and happiness. The more you hear it, the more you begin to believe it. Recite your affirmations daily, or several times throughout the day.

It is essential for you to have a healthy level of self-esteem. Now, that does not mean that you have to love EVERYTHING about yourself. We all have some things that we may want to tweak about ourselves. Having a healthy dose of self-esteem means being able to accept your flaws and yet still know that you have great value and worth.

Learn how to accept compliments. When you struggle with low self-worth, accepting compliments can be hard. This difficulty could stem from being a victim of emotional abuse. Constantly hearing demeaning and derogatory words used to describe you such as, "You're ugly," "You're stupid," "No one is ever going to love you," etc., can have an impact on your self-worth. Therefore, it can sometimes be hard to hear kind words, let alone believe the pleasant things that people are saying to you.

There are people in this world that are sincere and see your goodness; receiving compliments from them can help you feel good about yourself. Therefore, you need to work on accepting compliments instead of feeling unworthy or not believing them. While it may be hard at first to accept a compliment at face valuc, it does get easier the more often it happens. So just smile and say, "Thank you!"

Practice self-compassion. Self-compassion is being warm and understanding toward yourself when you make a mistake or feel inadequate, rather than discounting your pain or beating yourself up with self-criticism. Self-compassion is treating yourself kindly, accepting your strengths and imperfections, and treating yourself with the same thoughtfulness and support that you would show someone you genuinely care about.

When you feel good on the inside it shows on the outside. When you feel good about yourself things tend to flow more smoothly in your life. You tend to be healthier, happier, and more fulfilled. You deserve all of these and more!

CHAPTER 6

# Reconnecting

Trauma changes the way you see yourself and others, which can make it difficult to emotionally connect with others. It can also make it difficult to feel in touch with yourself. The aftermath of abuse and trauma can disrupt your sense of intimacy with yourself and others because your perception and sense of self have become distorted. What you thought you knew about yourself may have changed. You may not know how to identify your feelings or communicate your feelings. You may begin experiencing a range of emotions that are unfamiliar, which can cause you to feel confused or overwhelmed.

In order to protect yourself, you may begin to deny or even bury your feelings. You may go through life emotionally numb as a way of protecting yourself from emotional pain. When you are emotionally numb, you may feel a sense of safety and protection in the short term, however the long-term consequences can actually be harmful.

When you suppress or cut off your feelings, you are temporarily avoiding the painful feelings; however, you are also cutting off the good feelings, such as love, joy, peace, etc. It is necessary that you understand that ALL feelings are important. Your feelings are informational guides, designed to help you understand yourself. They are also a necessary part of connecting with others.

Despite what you may believe, your feelings do not permanently disappear when you bury them deep down inside. It may provide a temporary sense of relief, but it is ONLY temporary. You may be thinking to yourself right now, *What is wrong with that? At least I don't have to feel the hurt and the pain now.* The problem with this method is that eventually your feelings will come back up to the surface when you are triggered or provoked by something that reminds you of the abuse or trauma that you suffered. Those feelings will usually show up as anger or rage.

Another way that you may avoid your feelings of pain is by numbing them with drugs, alcohol, or other addictive behaviors, such as sex, food, or work. Learning to work through your feelings, instead of avoiding them, will put you on the right path toward healing. Identifying and recognizing your feelings and emotions are important parts of reconnecting. Reconnecting with yourself begins with knowing yourself. How well do you know yourself, your likes and dislikes? It's time for a self-inventory.

*Put a check next to the answers that apply to you.*

**Do you**

- ☐ know when you feel calm and relaxed?
- ☐ know when you feel satisfied?
- ☐ know when you feel dissatisfied?
- ☐ know when you feel angry?
- ☐ know when you feel frightened?
- ☐ know how to comfort yourself when upset?
- ☐ know when you need help?
- ☐ know you have a right to your own thoughts and feelings?
- ☐ know you have a right to express your thoughts and feelings?

Perhaps your past, your abuse, or your trauma caused you to give up trying to say what you really feel or want. As a survivor, you may have been in a situation where your voice was taken away from you or disregarded. It is important that you understand that your ability to speak your feelings and needs is empowering. If speaking aloud is a challenge for you, or feels like a high level of risk, then start with journaling. Writing in a journal is a safe way to begin expressing your thoughts and feelings. It does not matter if you are the only person who reads the journal. Journaling can be a powerful means of self-expression and self-understanding.

After you get in the habit of journaling, you will notice that you are becoming more comfortable expressing yourself and will then be motivated to move to the next level. When you are ready, begin expressing your feelings and wants aloud, this will help you to better reconnect with yourself and regain your voice.

Trauma can also create disconnection and disruption of intimacy in relationships. Some survivors tend to have difficulty forming and maintaining healthy relationships. People who have experienced abuse or trauma may see themselves as flawed or not worthy of being in an intimate relationship.

As a survivor, you may avoid relationships altogether. You may feel like you do not need anyone and, therefore, become excessively independent, constantly proving and proclaiming that you can do it all by yourself. Please be clear, there is nothing wrong with being independent. The issue is when you convince yourself that you do not need anything from anybody, EVER. This belief comes from the need to protect yourself from being hurt again, let down, or disappointed. The truth is we all need someone at some point in our lives. We were not created to go through this life all by ourselves.

As a way to protect yourself from past abusive relationships, you may not allow others to get close to you or get to know the real you. As a survivor, you may avoid intimacy in relationships or prematurely end relationships as soon as intimacy begins. Intimacy does not necessarily mean sex. There are other ways to share love and affection without sex. Recognizing this concept will help you to understand how a person can feel lonely and isolated while being engaged in a sexual relationship. Intimacy is about feeling emotionally connected and supported.

Intimacy can be physical, however, it is not just a physical act. There are other types of intimacy, such as emotional and spiritual. Emotional intimacy involves sharing authentic thoughts and feelings. It means feeling safe enough to share your deepest thoughts, your wildest dreams, as well as your worst fears. Spiritual intimacy involves shared beliefs, purpose, meaning, and inner peace. It is a deeper connection than thoughts and words. It is connecting through faith and prayer. The ability to intimately connect with others is another step toward healing.

Trauma can also cause you to isolate or avoid places, people, and activities that you once enjoyed. No matter what traumatic event or circumstance you endured, it is natural for the experience to affect your relationships with others. The belief that no one can understand you, or what you have gone through, separates you from the human connection. This disconnection can occur within families and friendships.

Oftentimes, the lack of understanding of the impact of trauma may cause family and friends to feel unsure about how to relate to you after your traumatic experience. They may even feel helpless, not knowing how to make you feel better.

Communication can break down as family members or friends struggle in their own way to come to terms with what happened to someone they love. As you are reading this book and learning more about yourself, it can be helpful to share with your family and friends how trauma has changed you and your view of the world. You may choose to keep the details of your trauma private, however, it will help to rebuild relationships if you share how trauma has changed you. When you feel comfortable enough and that the time is right, try opening up with your family and friends. As a survivor, the support and understanding of family and friends can be an essential source of healing.

It is important to understand that your body, mind, and spirit are all connected. Having a strong spiritual connection is a key component in the process of healing from abuse and trauma. Spirituality is a personal connection and a belief in something greater than yourself (i.e., God, a Higher Power). Spiritual comfort and strength can be obtained through prayer and meditation, which can add to your overall well-being. Spiritual connection moves you toward love, meaning, peace, hope, compassion, and wholeness.

Below are ways in which you can improve your spiritual health.

- Make some time in your life to do the things that help you grow spiritually, such as praying, meditating, singing devotional songs, reading inspirational books, attending religious services, having quiet time for thinking, spending time in nature, giving back to your community, or volunteering.

- Find things that bring you a sense of inner peace, comfort, love, and connection.

It is important for you to understand that reconnecting involves being able to take a low level of risk. This is the risk of being open and letting yourself be known to others. It also involves a level of acceptance; this means being able, and willing, to recognize acceptance from others when they offer it. Remember to take baby steps in this process. Go at your own pace. When you are feeling safe, you are progressing in the area of trust, and have begun noticing an increase in self-esteem, you will then know in your heart that you are ready to reconnect with others. It is vital that you value and respect yourself enough to listen to how you feel. Paying attention to yourself will provide you with the information you need to determine when you are ready to move forward.

# CHAPTER 7

# Healing

As you have experienced and survived abuse and trauma, it is never about what is wrong with you. It is about **what happened to you**. What you have gone through has changed you. It changed how you see yourself, others, and the world. Healing from trauma is a life-long process. It means moving towards hope. It means seeing yourself in a positive light. It means finding your strength and courage to create a new, healthier, and happier chapter of your life.

Healing from abuse and trauma is a journey. It is about learning healthy ways of releasing the pain of the past so that it no longer controls you and holds you captive. It is about feeling good about the life you are creating for yourself. Healing is a state of mind. It's when you have joy and peace and are able to have healthy and meaningful relationships. Healing also involves a transformational change, much like a caterpillar transforms into a butterfly. A butterfly is a symbol of renewal. Let's imagine a butterfly as we discuss the healing process.

The daily life for a caterpillar involves crawling on the ground, sometimes being unnoticed or having people look down on it. People make negative comments, *augh look at that caterpillar*. No one thinks the caterpillar is beautiful. Oftentimes, survivors of abuse go through similar experiences in their lives. They experience times of loneliness, fear, uncertainty, and being looked down on and judged by others. No one sees their beauty and, many times, they themselves do not feel beautiful.

Just like with a caterpillar, in order to move forward change *has to occur*. There are several phases involved in your journey toward healing.

*The Learning and Growing phase* – You begin to learn all you can about your experience. As a caterpillar sheds her old skin to adapt to her new growth, *you* learn and shed old beliefs that perhaps had you stuck or feeling trapped. During this phase, you learn more about your relationships, situations, and yourself. You begin to see things for what they really are. You may begin to encounter some level of fear or uncertainty, however, you recognize that you will need to do some things differently as a result of your newfound awareness.

*Is there something that is causing you to feel unsure about the road ahead? List the things that may be causing you to feel afraid or uncomfortable at this moment in your life.*

_____

_____

_____

Although change can be uncomfortable at times, not all change is bad. May you find comfort as you begin to move toward change and the growing phase.

**Declaration:** I declare I am prepared. I have what it takes to move toward change. I am learning and growing in ways that are beneficial to my healing and my life.

*The Grieving and Rebuilding phase* – This phase is painful, and it has its struggles. You may feel that you cannot go on. You need to grieve, rest, retreat, and rebuild. Just like the caterpillar finds rest and retreat in her cocoon. This phase takes time and effort.

*Is there something or someone that you need to grieve right now? Are there areas of your life that you need to rebuild? List them below.*

_____

_____

_____

Grief is a natural response to loss. You may have experienced many losses due to your abuse or trauma, such as a loss of your sense of self, a loss of independence, or even a physical loss. Allow yourself as much time as needed to grieve and rebuild.

**Declaration:** I declare I deserve better for myself and my life. I am no longer bound by grief, fear, or doubt.

*The Transformation phase* – This is where change and transforming takes place. It involves letting go of the old, while moving toward something new. It is during this phase that you learn how to transform your pain into fuel and opportunities for growth. You become emotionally present in your life, you change your negative beliefs, and you relinquish the past. Just as the caterpillar completes transformation in the cocoon.

*Are there any negative beliefs you need to let go of in this moment? List them below.*

_____

_____

_____

**Declaration:** I declare my attitude determines by altitude. I will turn my pain into my purpose.

*The Awakening or Emerging* phase – During this phase, the caterpillar emerges as a beautiful butterfly. She now has the ability to do things she never thought she could do. She is free to spread her wings and fly away. For you, *it's a time of breakthrough.* As you emerge, you will recognize certain gifts and talents that you did not know were deep inside of you. You will begin to recognize a new awareness of inner strength, a different set of priorities, heighted appreciation for life, and the confidence that you can survive anything.

I encourage you to begin seeing yourself from a strengths-based perspective. Begin reconstructing your perception of yourself and the meaning of life. This new perception does not mean that you discount or minimize your struggles, your pain, your abuse, your traumatic experiences, or your past in any way. It is about imagining your life and your future in a way in which you get to create. It is a time of discovery and personal growth.

*Can you identify any positive growth or new understanding in any areas of your life? Consider the following areas: personal strength, spiritual change, relationships with others, appreciation of life or new possibilities in life. List the areas that apply to you and how you have grown in each one.*

_____

_____

_____

_____

_____

_____

_____

The very fact that you have survived reflects your strength. You never did anything to cause what happened to you and you deserve to be happy and feel safe. What you went through is not who you are and does not define you.

It's time for you to heal. Healing is being able to reconnect with yourself, being able to embrace life by regaining a sense of control, rebuilding trust and bonds, and enjoying positive and healthy relationships. Healing is an individualized process and not necessarily a linear one. You may not experience healing in the exact same way as someone else. You may experience it in a different order or may need to revisit a stage. Please give yourself permission to move at your own pace and in your own way, one that is healthy for you.

*Well, how do I know when I'm healing?* Great question! When painful memories no longer take over your life, healing is occurring. When your past no longer defines you. When your quality of life improves on a daily basis. When you begin using what you have gone through to inspire yourself and help others, you are healing.

This book is ending, but this is not the end of your journey. Remember to use the effective tools that you learned throughout this book (grounding, journaling, self-compassion, etc.). Remember to allow the process of transformation to take place. The butterfly knows the right time to fly, no one has to tell it. You, too, will know the right time to fly with new wings of wisdom and courage and when it's your time to soar.

**Declaration:** I declare I will be patient with myself on this journey. I will love myself enough to continue this journey. I will fulfill my passion and purpose!

# References

*nimh.nih.gov* N.p., Web. 13 Nov. 2021.
<https://www.nimh.nih.gov/health/publications/post-traumatic-stress-disorder-ptsd

*psychdb.com.* N.p., Web. *24 Nov. 2021.*
<*https://www.psychdb.com/_media/grounding-techniques-provider-patient-handout.pdf*>.

*vetmed.wsu.edu.* N.p., Web. 18 Nov. 2021.
<https://www.vetmed.wsu.edu/docs/librariesprovider16/default-document-library/the-long-shadow-adult-survivors-of-childhood-abuse.pdf?sfvrsn=0>.

*winona.edu.* N.p., Web. 24 Nov. 2021.
<https://www.winona.edu/resilience/Media/Grounding-Worksheet.pdf>.

*womenshealth.gov* N.p., Web. 13 Nov. 2021.
<https://www.womenshealth.gov/relationships-and-safety/signs-abuse

# About the Author

Merry Ware is a wife and a mother of two daughters. Merry is a Licensed Professional Counselor, (LPC) and a National Certified Counselor (NCC). She is the founder and CEO of Survival 2 Victory, Inc. a behavioral health and wellness center for women. She has a Master's degree in Community Counseling, a Master's degree in Organizational Management and a Bachelor's degree in Communications. Merry is also a Continuing Education trainer. She provides training for mental health professionals through Continuing Education workshops and live webinars.

Merry is an advocate for female survivors of abuse and an inspirational speaker. She provides public speaking in communities, churches, and special events on topics such as Healing from Abuse, Women Empowerment, and Mental Health Awareness.

Merry is also a Licensed Minister. She is operating in her passion and purpose, which is to help hurting women heal. She recognizes the need to provide guidance, counseling, encouragement, education, and empowerment in order to transform the lives of female survivors of abuse.

**Website:** www.survival2victory.org
**Email:** info@survival2victory.org
**Facebook:** survival2victory.org
**Instagram:** survival2victory

His Glory Creations Publishing, LLC is an International Christian Book Publishing Company, which helps launch the creative fiction and non-fiction works of new, aspiring and seasoned authors across the globe, through stories that are inspirational, empowering, life-changing or educational in nature, including poetry, journals, children's books, and recipe books.

**DESIRE TO KNOW MORE?**
Contact Information:
CEO and Founder: Felicia C. Lucas
www.hisglorycreationspublishing.com
Email: hgcpublishingllc@gmail.com
Facebook: His Glory Creations Publishing (HGCPAC)
Instagram: Coach Felicia Lucas
Phone: 919-679-1706

Made in the USA
Columbia, SC
13 June 2022

61674033R00037